SOUTH RUTLAND
ELEMENTARY LIBRARY

# Dominican Republic

*Many Cultures, One World*

by Mary Englar

Consultant:
Ramona Hernández, Ph.D.
Director of CUNY Dominican Studies Institute
City College of New York
New York, New York

DISCARDED
SOUTH RUTLAND ELEMENTARY

## Blue Earth Books

an imprint of Capstone Press
Mankato, Minnesota

Blue Earth Books are published by Capstone Press
151 Good Counsel Drive, P.O. Box 669, Mankato, Minnesota 56002
*http://www.capstonepress.com*

Copyright © 2004 by Capstone Press. All rights reserved.

No part of this book may be reproduced in whole or in part, or stored in a retrieval system, or transmitted in any form
or by any means, electronic, mechanical, photocopying, recording, or otherwise, without written permission from the publisher.
For information regarding permission, write to Capstone Press, 151 Good Counsel Drive,
P.O. Box 669, Dept. R, Mankato, Minnesota 56002.
Printed in the United States of America

*Library of Congress Cataloging-in-Publication Data*
Englar, Mary.
    Dominican Republic / by Mary Englar.
    p. cm.—(Many cultures, one world)
    Includes bibliographical references and index.
    Contents: Welcome to the Dominican Republic—A Dominican legend—City and country life—Seasons in the Dominican
Republic—Family life in the Dominican Republic—Laws, rules, and customs—Pets in the Dominican Republic—Sights to see in the
Dominican Republic.
    ISBN 0-7368-2453-7 (hardcover)
    1. Dominican Republic—Juvenile literature. [1. Dominican Republic.] I. Title. II. Series.
F1934.2.E64 2004
972.93—dc22
                                          2003012127

**Editorial credits**
Editor: Megan Schoeneberger
Series Designer: Kia Adams
Photo Researcher: Alta Schaffer
Product Planning Editor: Eric Kudalis

**Cover photo**
Dominican Republic coastal view by Greg Johnston

**Artistic effects**
DigitalVision

**Photo credits**
Aurora/Tophoven/Laif, 24–25
Bruce Coleman Inc./Sullivan and Rogers, 6, 23
Capstone Press/Gary Sundermeyer, 3 (all), 15, 29, back cover
Corbis/Bradley Smith, 8–9; Tom Bean, 20, 27 (right)
Corbis Sygma/Amet Jean Pierre, 10; Diaro Listin, 17 (right);
    Giraud Phillippe, 28
Greg Johnston, 4–5, 14, 16–17
Houserstock/Steve Cohen, 13 (right), 21
Index Stock Imagery/Timothy O'Keefe, 9 (right); Volvox, 11
Mrs. Andres Redondo, 22 (bottom)
One Mile Up Inc., 22 (top)
S. Blair Hedges/Penn State, 25 (right)
TRIP/Tibor Bognar, 26–27
The Viesti Collection Inc./Martha Cooper, 18–19, 19 (right);
    Peter Purchia, 12–13

1 2 3 4 5 6 09 08 07 06 05 04

# Contents

*Chapter 1*
Welcome to the Dominican Republic ........... 4

*Chapter 2*
A Dominican Legend ..................... 8

*Chapter 3*
City and Country Life ........................ 12

*Chapter 4*
Seasons in the Dominican Republic ............. 16

*Chapter 5*
Family Life in the Dominican Republic .......... 18

*Chapter 6*
Laws, Rules, and Customs ..................... 22

*Chapter 7*
Pets in the Dominican Republic ................ 24

*Chapter 8*
Sights to See in the Dominican Republic ....... 26

Glossary ................................. 30
Read More ............................... 30
Useful Addresses ......................... 31
Internet Sites ............................ 31
Index .................................... 32

**Turn to page 7 to find a map of the Dominican Republic.**

**See page 15 to learn how to make a favorite Dominican drink.**

**Check out page 21 to learn how to play a Dominican game.**

**Look on page 29 to find out how to make amber soap.**

CHAPTER 1

# Welcome to the Dominican Republic

Visitors to Lake Enriquillo watch for crocodiles and other wildlife. Along the shore, pink flamingos and other birds search for their morning meals. Nearby, crocodiles soak up sunlight. By afternoon, the crocodiles swim into deeper water to escape the heat.

In the middle of the lake is Isla Cabritos. Many strange animals live in this island's brush. Rhinoceros iguanas have horns on their faces. Another rare iguana has red eyes and a sharp tail.

Many birds nest near the shore of Lake Enriquillo. Lake Enriquillo is the largest lake in the Dominican Republic.

# Facts about the Dominican Republic

Name:................Dominican Republic
Capital:..............Santo Domingo
Population:.........about 9 million people
Size:...................18,815 square miles
              (48,730 square kilometers)
Language: .........Spanish
Religions:...........Roman Catholic (95 percent),
              other (5 percent)
Highest point: ....Pico Duarte, 10,417 feet
              (3,175 meters) above sea level
Lowest point:.....Lake Enriquillo, 151 feet
              (46 meters) below sea level
Main crops: .......Sugarcane, coffee, cotton,
              cocoa, tobacco, rice, beans
Money:..............Dominican peso

The Dominican Republic is in the West Indies. The Dominican Republic shares the island of **Hispaniola** with Haiti. Three mountain ranges cross the border with Haiti. The Sierra de Neiba and the Sierra de Bahoruco are in the southwest. The peaks of Cordillera Central cut through the middle of the country. The country also has deserts, thick forests, and nearly 800 miles (1,290 kilometers) of coastline.

Forests grow on the slopes of the Sierra de Neiba. Farmers have cut down many of the trees.

CHAPTER 2

# A Dominican Legend

The first people on Hispaniola were the Taíno (ty-EE-no) Indians. They also lived in present-day Cuba and Puerto Rico.

The Taíno Indians tell many stories about the sea. Legends are stories that explain something to people. They are often based on fact but are not completely true. The following legend tells how the sea formed.

The Dominican Republic has a long coastline. The Taíno Indians lived along the coast before explorers arrived.

Taíno Indians carved this large rock sculpture in the Dominican Republic.

# How the Sea Began

A long time ago, there was no sea. The Great Spirit, Yaya, and his wife lived on the land. Every day, they worked in their garden with their son. Yaya's son was polite. He always helped his father.

The son grew up. He did not like his father telling him what to do anymore. Yaya and his son argued all the time. One day, Yaya fought with his son. Before they could forgive each other, his son died. Yaya and his wife were very sad.

Yaya put his son's bones in a **gourd** from a **calabash tree**. He hung the gourd from the roof of his house. Yaya and his wife tried to forget about their son. A long time passed. Still, Yaya missed his son. One day, he told his wife to get the gourd. He wanted to see his son's bones.

Yaya and his wife looked in the gourd. The bones were gone. In their place, fish filled the gourd. The fish looked tasty. Yaya and his wife ate some. Each time they ate one fish, another appeared. It was a magic gourd.

*The Taino Indians made containers from gourds of the calabash tree.*

One day a boy watched as Yaya put away the gourd. The boy wondered what made this gourd so special. He waited until Yaya and his wife went to their garden. He crept into their house and took down the gourd. The boy saw that it was full of fish. He ate one, and then he ate more and more.

Soon the boy heard Yaya and his wife returning. He jumped up and quickly tried to hang the gourd. He slipped. The gourd fell to the ground and broke. Water rushed out of the gourd. It filled the house with water and fish. Water spilled out of Yaya's house and across the land.

The water covered the earth with rivers and lakes. Still, it came rushing out. Fish filled the lakes and rivers. Finally, water surrounded all of the land. And this is how the sea began.

Bright, colorful fish swam from Yaya's magic gourd. Today, many fish swim in the ocean around the Dominican Republic.

11

CHAPTER 3

# City and Country Life

About one-half of the Dominican people live outside of cities. Most of these people are farmers. They grow food for their families and sell the extra food at the market. They work on large **sugarcane** farms and cattle ranches.

Most families in the country live in small houses. These houses are painted bright colors. One wall might be orange, and another might be purple. Many country houses do not have electricity or running water.

Some farmers use horses to plow their fields.

Brightly painted houses add color to the countryside.

Many people have moved from the country to Santo Domingo, Puerto Plata, Monte Cristi, and other cities to find work. People in cities often work in factories or office buildings. Other people become students or artists. In cities near the ocean, many people fish.

In cities, most people live in small apartments. Large cities do not have enough housing for everyone. Outside the cities, people build houses with cardboard and tin. These families sell food on the street or shine shoes. Some people work as maids or gardeners.

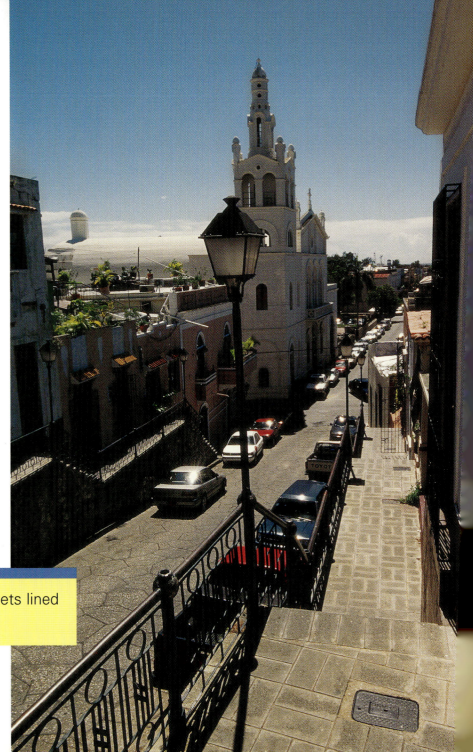

Santo Domingo has narrow streets lined with old buildings.

# Morir Soñando

Fresh fruit is grown in the Dominican Republic. Dominicans enjoy fresh bananas, coconuts, and pineapples. They also enjoy lemons, limes, oranges, grapefruit, and other citrus fruits.

Cold juices are popular on hot days. In this recipe, the drink's Spanish name, *morir soñando*, means "to die dreaming." This fruit shake is made with orange juice and milk. The amount of sugar you need depends on the juice's tartness.

## What You Need

### Ingredients
½ cup (120 mL) crushed ice
½ cup (120 mL) fresh orange juice
1 tablespoon (15 mL) sugar
½ cup (120 mL) milk

### Equipment
dry-ingredient measuring cups
blender
liquid measuring cup
drinking glass

## What You Do

1. Pour ice into the blender. With an adult's help, use the blender to crush the ice into small pieces.
2. Add the orange juice, sugar, and milk to ice in the blender.
3. Blend the ingredients until they are creamy.
4. Pour into a glass and enjoy.

Makes 1 serving

CHAPTER 4

# Seasons in the Dominican Republic

The Dominican Republic's rainy seasons differ by area. The rainy season in the north lasts from October until May. The south and southeast have a rainy season from May to October.

Most of the Dominican Republic is hot throughout the year. Plants grow well in the **tropical** air. The rain waters the sugarcane, palm trees, and banana trees.

Different plants grow in drier parts of the country. Coffee is grown in mountain valleys. Only cactuses and thorn trees grow in the deserts.

Many types of plants, such as palm trees and ferns, grow in the Dominican Republic's wet, warm air.

# Hurricanes

Huge storms called **hurricanes** often strike the Dominican Republic. These storms have strong winds. Hurricanes can harm the land, crops, animals, and cities.

In 1998, Hurricane Georges hit the Dominican Republic. For 16 hours, the storm moved slowly across the country. By the time it was over, more than 200 people had died. Dominicans are still fixing houses and roads damaged in this storm.

In 1998, Hurricane Georges flattened many homes in the Dominican Republic.

CHAPTER 5

# Family Life in the Dominican Republic

Dominicans keep strong family ties. Grandparents, aunts, uncles, cousins, parents, and children often share one house. When people move away, they stay in touch with their families. They send money, letters, and gifts home.

Families usually gather for lunch. This meal is the largest meal of the day. Almost all Dominicans eat rice and beans for lunch. Some families also have stewed chicken, pork, or goat meat. Others add vegetables and fruits. Family members talk and joke while they eat. Lunch often lasts two hours.

Many Dominican families enjoy playing games together.

## Birthdays

On their birthdays, Dominican children invite their friends and families to a party. Richer families sometimes hire a **merengue** band. Everyone enjoys dancing to the lively music.

Sunday is a day to enjoy family and friends. Many families dress up in their best clothes. Some go to church. After church, they meet friends in town. They walk together and catch up on the news.

In the evening, some people go home for supper. Other people stay out with their friends. They watch a baseball game or play dominoes.

## Baseball

Baseball is the national sport of the Dominican Republic. From October until February, teams play in every city. The games are almost always sold out. Children play baseball for fun wherever there is space for a game. Many young boys want to play baseball when they grow up.

Many baseball teams from the United States run training camps for young Dominican players. If the players do well, they might play in the United States. Sammy Sosa, Alex Rodriguez, and many other Dominicans play baseball in the United States.

Dominicans of all ages enjoy a game of baseball.

# El Cartero

Dominican children play many games besides baseball. They may play *el cartero* at a birthday party. *El cartero* is Spanish for "the postman." You can play this game with your friends.

## What You Need

at least 8 players
one chair for each player

## What You Do

1. Arrange all chairs but one in a circle. Put the last chair in the middle of the circle. Make sure players have enough room to move between the chairs and around the outside of the circle.
2. Choose one player to start in the middle. The other players sit in the chairs that are arranged in a circle.
3. The player in the middle says, "Someone came by my house."
4. The other players ask, "Who?"
5. The middle player answers, "The postman."
6. The other players ask, "What did he bring?"
7. The middle player answers, "Letters."
8. The rest ask, "For whom?"
9. The middle player answers with a statement that describes some of the other players in the group. "All the boys," or "girls wearing blue," or "kids who like bananas" are some examples of statements that the player may make.
10. The players who fit the description must jump up and find a new seat. The middle player also must find a seat in the circle.
11. One player will not find a new seat. He or she becomes the middle player. The game begins again.

CHAPTER 6

# Laws, Rules, and Customs

The Dominican Republic is a **democracy**. The people vote for their leaders. Dominicans elect a president and a vice president. They also vote for leaders to represent them in the senate and the chamber of deputies.

Children in the Dominican Republic must go to school until they are 14 years old. Students' families must pay for books, supplies, and uniforms. To save money, some students share books.

A white cross divides the Dominican flag. One blue and one red square is on each side. The blue stands for peace. The red stands for the blood of freedom fighters. The cross stands for the Roman Catholic faith. At the middle of the flag is the Dominican Republic's coat of arms.

Dominican money is called Dominican pesos. Each peso equals 100 centavos. Both coins and paper money are used.

The Dominican Republic celebrates Independence Day on February 27. The country became free from Haiti on that day in 1844. Women, men, children, soldiers, and police officers march in parades. The president gives a speech on TV. Flags fly along the streets.

Many Dominicans are Roman Catholic. Roman Catholics follow the teachings of Jesus Christ. Their leader, the pope, lives in Rome. Many Dominican holidays are based on the Roman Catholic faith.

Each year, Dominicans celebrate **carnival** the week before Lent. Carnival includes many parades with floats. Some people dance and sing in the streets. Some wear costumes and masks and walk in the parades.

Parades and costumes are part of the Dominican Republic's celebration of Independence Day.

CHAPTER 7

# Pets in the Dominican Republic

Many Dominicans keep pets. Dogs, cats, and parakeets are popular pets. Dominicans buy pets at outdoor markets or from pet shops in the cities. In the country, most families have a dog.

In some small towns, stray cats and dogs roam the streets. The homeless animals beg for food. The animals are unhealthy. Dominicans hope to solve the problem of homeless animals.

Children who live in the country take care of farm animals in addition to pet dogs.

## The Jaragua Lizard

In 1998, two scientists discovered the world's smallest lizard on an island off the coast of the Dominican Republic. The Jaragua lizard can curl up on a U.S. dime. It is less than 1 inch (2.5 centimeters) from head to tail. The lizard eats ants, spiders, and other insects.

*CHAPTER 8*

# Sights to See in the Dominican Republic

Santo Domingo, the capital city, is the oldest European city in the Americas. The Spanish founded the city in 1496. They built the Fortress of Santo Domingo and the Ozama Fortress in 1505. They wanted to protect the city from enemies and pirates. The forts have walls that are 6 feet (2 meters) thick. From the top of the forts, people can see both Santo Domingo and the sea.

The Dominican Republic has many tall mountains and green valleys. Pico Duarte is the tallest mountain in the West Indies.

People can still visit the Fortress of Santo Domingo to see how the Spanish defended their city from enemies and pirates.

Hikers use donkeys to carry heavy loads while they climb Pico Duarte.

Many visitors climb to the top. On a clear day, people can see the Atlantic Ocean to the north and the Caribbean Sea to the south.

Every year, humpback whales come to waters north of the Dominican Republic. The whales swim almost 4,000 miles (6,437 kilometers) from the North Atlantic Ocean to give birth. Scientists come from all around the world to study the whales. Tour boats take people out to watch the whales. The whales slap their tails against the water. They also jump into the air.

Tourists and scientists come to watch humpback whales north of the Dominican Republic.

# Making Amber Soap

The Dominican Republic has large amounts of a gem called amber. Amber comes from a sticky material made by some trees. The material is called resin. The resin hardens over millions of years. Some amber in the Dominican Republic is 20 to 30 million years old.

Some pieces of amber have whole insects, leaves, lizards, and frogs trapped inside. These plants and animals are also millions of years old. Amber allows scientists to study what life was like millions of years ago.

Melted soap hardens as it cools. You can use soap to preserve leaves, flowers, and other small objects.

## What You Need

butter knife
bar of orange-colored glycerin soap
small disposable microwave-safe container
microwave
toothpicks or craft sticks
small leaves, flowers, or plastic bugs

## What You Do

1. With an adult's help, carefully cut off about one-third of bar from end of soap. Cut this piece into smaller pieces so they will melt.
2. Place soap pieces in small microwave-safe container.
3. Microwave on low for about 20 seconds or until soap melts to a liquid.
4. Carefully remove container from microwave. Soap will be very hot. Use a toothpick or craft stick to stir the soap. Make sure all the chunks of soap have melted.
5. Quickly drop leaves, flowers, or plastic bugs into the soap. Use a toothpick or craft stick to push the items into the liquid soap. Be careful not to touch the hot soap.
6. Let the soap sit for at least one hour until it hardens.
7. Once the soap is hard, carefully bend the container until the soap loosens and falls out.

# Glossary

**calabash tree** (KAL-uh-bash TREE)—a type of tree that produces hard, round fruit called gourds

**carnival** (KAR-nuh-vuhl)—a celebration before the Christian period of Lent

**democracy** (di-MOK-ruh-see)—a type of government where people vote for their leaders

**gourd** (GORD)—a fruit with hard, dry shells often used for cups and bowls

**Hispaniola** (hiss-pan-YOH-lah)—an island shared by the Dominican Republic and Haiti; Hispaniola is the second largest island in the Caribbean; the first European city in the New World was started there.

**hurricane** (HUR-uh-kane)—a strong wind and rain storm that starts on the ocean

**merengue** (may-RAYN-gay)–fast, rhythmic music; the merengue is also a dance.

**sugarcane** (SHUG-ur-kayn)—a tall grass that has sugar in its woody stems

**tropical** (TROP-uh-kuhl)—warm and wet

# Read More

**Conley, Kate A.** *Dominican Republic.* The Countries. Edina, Minn.: Abdo, 2000.

**Dubois, Muriel L.** *Dominican Republic.* Countries of the World. Mankato, Minn.: Bridgestone Books, 2001.

**Temple, Bob.** *Dominican Republic.* Discovering the Caribbean. Philadelphia: Mason Crest, 2004.

## Useful Addresses

**Dominican Republic Tourist Board**
136 East 57 Street Suite 803
New York, NY 10022

**Embassy of the Dominican Republic in Canada**
130 Albert Street, Suite 418
Ottawa, Ontario KIP 5G4
Canada

**Embassy of the Dominican Republic in the United States**
1715 22nd Street NW
Washington, DC 20008

## Internet Sites

FactHound offers a safe, fun way to find Internet sites related to this book. All of the sites on FactHound have been researched by our staff.

### Here's how:

1. Visit *www.facthound.com*
2. Type in this special code **0736824537** for age-appropriate sites.
   Or enter a search word related to this book for a more general search.
3. Click on the **Fetch It** button.

**FactHound will fetch the best sites for you!**

# Index

amber, 29

baseball, 20
birthday, 19, 21

carnival, 23
celebrations, 19, 23
coastline, 6, 8
crops, 5, 16, 17

desert, 6, 16

Enriquillo, Lake, 4, 5

family, 12, 14, 18, 19, 20, 24
farming, 6, 12, 16
flag, 22
food, 12, 14, 15, 18
forests, 6
Fortress of Santo Domingo, 26, 27

government, 22

Hispaniola, 6, 8
holidays, 23
housing, 12, 13, 14, 17, 18
Hurricane Georges, 17

Independence Day, 23

language, 5
legend, 8, 10, 11

merengue, 19
money, 5, 22
Monte Cristi, 14
mountain, 6, 16, 26

Ozama Fortress, 26

pets, 24, 25
Pico Duarte, 5, 26, 27, 28
plants, 10, 16, 17
population, 5
Puerto Plata, 14

religion, 5, 22, 23

Santo Domingo, 5, 14, 26
school, 22
seasons, 16

Taíno Indians, 8, 9, 10

weather, 16, 17
wildlife, 4, 5, 11, 25, 28

SOUTH RUTLAND
ELEMENTARY LIBRARY